SIMPLIFIED GUIDE ON

LIFE COACHING AND GOAL SETTING

Empower Yourself, Achieve Your Dreams, And Master The Art Of Goal Setting With Proven Strategies For Success And Fulfillment

DR. ARIYA REYNA

CONTENTS

DISCLIAMER

This book is intended for informational purposes only and is not a substitute for professional medical advice, diagnosis, or treatment. The information provided in this book is based on the author's research and personal experiences and is not meant to replace the advice of healthcare professionals.

Readers are encouraged to consult with their healthcare providers before beginning any new exercise, wellness, or health program.

The author and publisher of this book are not responsible for any specific health or allergy needs that may require medical supervision and are not liable for any damages or negative consequences from any treatment, action, application, or preparation, to any person reading or following the information in this book.

The content of this book is not intended to be a substitute for professional medical advice, diagnosis, or treatment. Always seek the advice of your physician or other qualified health provider with any questions you may have regarding a medical condition.

The author and publisher disclaim responsibility for any adverse effects that may result from the use or application of the information contained in this book.

References to specific products, services, or organizations do not imply endorsement or recommendation by the author or the publisher.

The inclusion of such references is for illustrative purposes only. Thank you for reading and respecting the terms outlined in this disclaimer.

CHAPTER ONE

An Overview Of Life Coaching

Life coaching is a transforming process that helps people reach their full potential, develop and achieve meaningful objectives, and negotiate life's problems with clarity and purpose. Life coaching, which is based on a client-centered approach, focuses on self-discovery, personal growth, and making good adjustments in many parts of life. Unlike therapy, which frequently focuses on past troubles and emotional healing, life coaching is focused on the future, trying to unleash an individual's potential and assist them toward a more satisfying future.

Life coaches, who are qualified professionals with a wide range of talents, provide clients seeking personal and professional development help, encouragement, and critical criticism. The coaching relationship is based on trust and collaboration, which allows individuals to examine their values, strengths, and goals. Life coaches assist clients in gaining insights, setting realistic objectives, and developing concrete strategies to attain achievement via effective communication and strong questioning.

Understanding The Fundamentals Of Goal Setting

Goal setting is an essential component of personal and professional growth, acting as a guidepost for individuals as they pursue their dreams and objectives. An organized procedure that translates broad wants into precise, measurable, attainable, relevant, and time-bound (SMART) objectives is required for effective goal formulation. This strategy gives clarity and a measurable framework for success.

1. Specific: Clearly outline the aim, addressing the what, why, and how questions. The more explicit the aim, the easier it is to devise a strategy.

2. Measurable: Create criteria for tracking progress. Metrics, timelines, and other tangible measures of performance might be included.

3. Achievable: Make sure the aim is both practical and reachable. Individuals should be challenged by their objectives, but they should also be achievable.

4. Relevant: Align the aim with personal beliefs and long-term goals. A relevant aim is important and contributes to a broader goal.

5. Time-Bound: Establish a deadline for completing the goal. This provides a sense of urgency and helps people stay focused on their goals.

Life coaches are essential in assisting people through the goal-setting process. They help customers explain their goals, break them down into doable goals, and refine them to correspond with their beliefs and life vision.

A Life Coach's Role In Goal Setting

Life coaches serve as change agents, aiding people in establishing and achieving their objectives with clarity and confidence. Their responsibilities include several areas of the goal-setting process:

1. Clarifying objectives: Life coaches assist clients in articulating their objectives, ensuring that they are explicit, relevant, and in line with their beliefs. Coaches support individuals in understanding their wants and ambitions via active listening and deliberate questioning.

2. Developing Action Plans: Once goals have been established, life coaches work with clients to design actionable plans. This is breaking down major goals into smaller, more achievable tasks, identifying priorities, and addressing potential roadblocks.

3. Accountability: Accountability is a critical component of goal success. Life coaches provide constant encouragement and support while holding clients accountable for their commitments. Individuals can stay on track and motivated with regular check-ins and progress reviews.

4. Overcoming Obstacles: Life coaches help clients navigate obstacles and disappointments. Coaches give skills and tactics to overcome hurdles and

sustain momentum, whether it's addressing limiting beliefs, managing time efficiently, or overcoming the fear of failure.

5. Appreciating Success: Recognizing and appreciating accomplishments, no matter how minor, is critical for motivation. Life coaches urge their clients to recognize their accomplishments and reflect on the good adjustments they've achieved.

The Advantages Of Life Coaching In Achieving Goals

The collaboration of a life coach and a person seeking personal or professional progress has several advantages:

1. Clarity: Life coaching is an organized process for self-discovery that assists individuals in gaining clarity about their values, strengths, and objectives. This clarity lays the groundwork for developing meaningful goals.

2. Enhanced Focus: With the assistance of a life coach, individuals may prioritize their goals and

focus on the tasks required for success. This increased concentration reduces distractions and encourages effective use of time and energy.

3. Improved Confidence: Setting and attaining objectives with the help of a life coach increases confidence. Individuals build a sense of self-assurance that transcends beyond the precise goals they are pursuing when they see their progress and conquer hurdles.

4. Responsibility: Life coaches give a degree of responsibility that is difficult to accomplish on one's own. Knowing that someone is involved in their accomplishment encourages people to stick to their ambitions.

5. Life coaching stresses holistic growth, taking into account numerous facets of an individual's life such as profession, relationships, health, and personal well-being. This all-encompassing strategy guarantees that objectives contribute to overall life pleasure.

In conclusion, life coaching may be a great motivator for those who want to attain their goals. The coaching relationship's collaborative and forward-focused orientation, along with the concepts of successful goal planning, gives a framework for long-term personal and professional improvement.

Setting Smart Objectives

Setting SMART objectives is a strategic technique that improves goal attainment by offering a clear and disciplined framework. The SMART criteria guarantee that objectives are clear, measurable, attainable, relevant, and time-bound, providing a road map to achievement.

1. Specific: Define the purpose clearly, leaving no space for misunderstanding. Rather than a broad aim like "improve fitness," a more particular goal would be "exercise for 30 minutes five days a week."

2. Measurable: Create clear criteria for monitoring development. Measurable objectives include quantifiable aspects that allow individuals to

objectively judge their progress. For instance, "lose 10 pounds" is a measurable objective.

3. Achievable: Make sure the aim is both practical and reachable. While objectives should be hard, they should also be achievable. Setting an achievable objective entails taking into account one's resources, talents, and limits.

4. Relevant: Align the aim with larger goals and personal beliefs. A meaningful aim contributes to an individual's overall vision for their life. It should be meaningful to the individual.

5. Time-Bound: Establish a deadline for completing the goal. A time-bound objective fosters motivation and attention by creating a feeling of urgency. Instead of declaring "learn a new language," for example, a time-bound aim would be to "learn basic conversational skills in Spanish within three months."

Individuals are guided by life coaches in applying the SMART criteria to their objectives, ensuring that each target is carefully constructed for maximum impact. Individuals obtain a clear roadmap that improves motivation, responsibility, and overall performance by incorporating these ideas into the goal-setting process. Setting SMART objectives, along with the guidance of a qualified life coach, maybe a transforming path towards a more rewarding and purposeful existence, whether pursuing personal growth, job success, or increased well-being.

Making A Vision Board To Help You Visualize Your Goals

Creating a vision board is a strong technique for goal visualization in the domain of life coaching. A vision board is a visual depiction of one's hopes, desires, and objectives. It acts as a physical reminder of the anticipated future, integrating images, phrases, and symbols that correspond to the intended goals. This process involves both the conscious and subconscious minds, reaffirming the dedication to the goals specified.

A vision board works on the law of attraction, which states that ideas and energies attract comparable events. Individuals immerse themselves in a positive mentality by routinely examining the vision board, and developing a connection between their current behaviors and future objectives. This visual tool promotes clarity and concentration, directing individuals with fresh purpose toward their goals.

It is critical to examine all parts of life while creating a vision board, including personal, professional, and emotional components. Choosing pictures and statements that elicit strong emotions improves the board's efficacy, making the visualizing experience more vivid. Life coaches frequently accompany their clients through this process, allowing a deeper investigation of values, interests, and long-term goals.

CHAPTER TWO

Overcoming Obstacles And Difficulties In Goal Accomplishment

Obstacles and hurdles are unavoidable when pursuing any aim. Life coaching provides individuals with the tools and mentality required to successfully handle these obstacles. One critical factor is to reframe problems as chances for progress. A professional life coach assists individuals in viewing failures as opportunities to learn, adapt, and progress rather than as impediments.

Overcoming hurdles frequently necessitates a mix of tenacity, problem-solving abilities, and an optimistic attitude. Life coaches work with clients to create a personalized approach to dealing with issues. This may entail breaking down major goals into smaller, more achievable activities, developing a step-by-step action plan, and anticipating probable roadblocks.

Individuals can psychologically and emotionally prepare for the path ahead by anticipating problems.

Furthermore, life coaching highlights the need to get help. Building a strong social network or getting expert help, having a support system is essential for overcoming obstacles. Coaches promote open communication and teach individuals how to properly harness their resources.

Increasing Self-Efficacy And Confidence

Confidence is essential for goal success, and life coaching may help you acquire and maintain it. A life coach assists individuals in recognizing and celebrating their talents and accomplishments, so building a good self-image. Individuals get the confidence to face new obstacles by appreciating earlier triumphs.

Confidence is directly related to self-efficacy or belief in one's capacity to achieve. Life coaches assist clients in identifying and challenging limiting beliefs that may be impeding their success. Individuals can reframe negative thinking patterns through focused exercises and reflective practices, replacing them with empowering ideas that boost their feeling of self-efficacy.

Setting attainable goals is another important method for boosting confidence. Life coaches help clients set realistic, quantifiable objectives, assuring a constant stream of success along the way. Each achievement acts as a stepping stone toward increased self-assurance and a stronger conviction in one's skills.

Creating A Growth Mindset

The notion of a development mindset is central to the philosophy of life coaching. A growth mindset, as defined by psychologist Carol Dweck, is the concept that talents and intellect can be developed through devotion and hard effort. Life coaches highlight the necessity of viewing problems as learning and growth opportunities rather than fixed markers of one's capabilities.

Failures must be reframed as learning experiences to develop a growth mindset. Individuals are guided by life coaches to accept losses as useful lessons, helping them to understand what went wrong and how they might do better in the future. This adjustment in outlook fosters resilience and the resolve to continue in the face of adversity.

Furthermore, life coaching uses the power of positive affirmations and self-talk to help people establish a development mindset. Individuals may modify their thought patterns over time by intentionally choosing affirmations that strengthen their conviction in their ability to learn and adapt. This deliberate emphasis on positive self-talk helps to a mindset in which setbacks are viewed as stepping stones rather than insurmountable hurdles.

Time Management And Goal Achievement

Effective time management is a critical component in the pursuit of goals. Life coaching provides individuals with ways to optimize their time and energy, allowing them to make regular progress toward their goals. Prioritization is a crucial notion that assists customers in identifying and focusing on tasks that are most directly related to their goals.

In time management, creating a realistic and well-structured timetable is critical. Life coaches help people break down bigger goals into practical stages, assigning time for each activity. This method not only increases productivity but also reduces the chance of feeling overwhelmed.

Life coaching also highlights the significance of adaptation in time management. Circumstances might shift, and unexpected obstacles can develop. Coaches educate customers on how to change their plans while staying focused on the end objective. Flexibility is an essential talent for handling the ever-changing nature of life and work.

Finally, life coaching gives an all-encompassing framework for individuals to create and attain their goals. Life coaching provides a complete approach to personal and professional development, from the beginning phases of establishing a vision board to overcoming barriers, increasing confidence, developing a growth mindset, and mastering time management. Individuals who participate in this transforming process not only improve their goal-setting abilities but also develop a mentality that drives them toward a more meaningful and prosperous future.

Goal Setting Requires Effective Communication Skills

Communication is essential in the goal-setting process, particularly in the field of life coaching. A life coach acts as a guide, assisting clients in articulating their goals and developing a plan to accomplish them. Successful communication is a must for success.

To begin, a life coach must be able to actively listen. The coach develops a thorough knowledge of the client's viewpoint by carefully listening to their thoughts, desires, and concerns. This not only builds trust but also enables the coach to personalize their advice to the client's specific requirements. A coach can uncover possible hurdles or limiting attitudes that may impede goal fulfillment by actively listening.

Furthermore, successful communication within goal setting requires the ability to question. Clients are encouraged to examine their ideas and motives by asking open-ended questions.

A life coach can help clients discover hidden aspirations or reveal deeper meanings by delving into the why behind a goal. This introspective approach not only improves the goals but also strengthens the client's commitment to the trip ahead.

Furthermore, communication clarity is critical. A life coach must communicate information in a clear and intelligible way, ensuring that the client understands the procedures necessary to achieve their goals.

Miscommunications might result in misplaced efforts and frustration.

As a result, a life coach's ability to reduce complicated ideas into basic, achievable steps is a critical communication skill.

CHAPTER THREE

Values Identification And Alignment With Goals

Goals that align with an individual's basic beliefs are more likely to be pursued with zeal and dedication. Life coaching entails assisting clients in identifying and aligning their values with their goals, resulting in a powerful synergy that promotes motivation and resilience.

The first step is to learn about the client's basic values. A life coach may utilize a variety of activities and talks to help the client discover what is genuinely important to them. Understanding values enables the coach to direct the client toward objectives that are both externally desired and internally satisfying.

Once determined, the connection of values and goals gives the pursuit a feeling of purpose. When a goal is aligned with a client's sincerely held values, it transforms into a meaningful undertaking that fosters intrinsic drive. This passion transforms into a driving force that propels the client through difficulties and disappointments.

Furthermore, matching values and goals improves decision-making. When confronted with goal-related decisions, the client can use their values as a compass. This alignment guarantees that the objective is pursued by the client's real self, eliminating internal tensions and generating a sense of authenticity.

Celebrating Achievements And Successes

Celebrating milestones and triumphs is an important component of reaching objectives that is frequently overlooked. Life coaching emphasizes the importance of recognizing progress to maintain momentum and cultivate a positive mindset.

Celebrating achievements gives you a psychological lift. It enables people to acknowledge their accomplishments, confirming their sense that they are capable of conquering obstacles. This positive reinforcement boosts self-esteem and confidence, both of which are important factors in maintaining motivation.

Life coaches frequently advise clients to create smaller, attainable milestones along the way to greater goals. Celebrating these small accomplishments turns the trip into a succession of victories, making the ultimate objective appear more realistic. This method also aids in breaking down a seemingly impossible undertaking into small parts, decreasing overwhelm.

Furthermore, marking anniversaries generates a positive feedback cycle. The pleasure and satisfaction felt when making progress are significant motivators. This optimism flows over into the next stage of goal attainment, pulling folks onward with fresh vigor and passion.

Goals Are Evaluated And Adjusted As Needed.

Goal-setting flexibility is a feature of good life coaching. While objectives offer a sense of direction, life is fluid, and circumstances can shift. A good life coach walks clients through the process of evaluating and if required, revising objectives to correspond with changing circumstances.

Regular evaluations are essential for measuring progress and identifying areas that may require improvement. Assessments entail weighing both the concrete results and the client's subjective experience. This comprehensive strategy guarantees that changes take into account not just external accomplishments but also the client's well-being and happiness.

Changing goals does not signify failure; rather, it shows adaptation and resilience. Life coaches help clients reevaluate their objectives in light of new knowledge, shifting priorities, or unexpected setbacks. This technique promotes a growth mindset by highlighting the necessity of learning from experiences and adapting strategies as needed.

The Connection Between Habits And Goal Achievement

Habits play a critical role in goal achievement. Life coaching acknowledges that establishing good habits that are aligned with the intended goals is frequently required for long-term change. Understanding the connection between habits and goal achievement is critical for good coaching.

For starters, habits give a defined framework for achieving goals. They reduce the cognitive strain involved with decision-making by automating actions. Life coaches encourage a smoother and more lasting path toward achievement by assisting clients in establishing habits that match their goals.

Furthermore, habits help with consistency. Goals are rarely attained by irregular attempts, but rather through constant, repeated acts. Life coaches assist clients in developing habits that become established in their daily routine, assuring consistent and dependable progress toward the intended results.

Breaking down major ambitions into smaller, achievable habits is a frequent life coaching method for goal fulfillment. This method not only streamlines the procedure but also increases the chances of success. Clients can achieve gradual improvements, creating momentum over time, by concentrating on adopting certain behaviors.

Finally, good communication, value alignment, milestone celebrations, goal assessment and adjustment, and recognizing the link between habits and goal accomplishment are all essential components of life coaching. These ideas combine to build a complete framework that enables people to define and achieve meaningful objectives, promoting personal growth and fulfillment. Life coaching, with its emphasis on these concepts, helps people live a more meaningful and deliberate life.

CHAPTER FOUR

Methods For Staying Motivated Throughout The Journey

Life coaching is an exciting way to go on a path of self-improvement and goal attainment. However, maintaining motivation along this trip might be difficult. To overcome this, life coaches use a variety of tactics to keep people motivated and dedicated to their goals.

One important method is to divide larger goals into smaller, more doable activities. The sensation of success gained from accomplishing these tiny chores serves as a constant source of inspiration. Life coaches frequently collaborate with clients to develop a roadmap, defining milestones to assist in measuring progress and celebrating accomplishments along the way.

Another successful strategy is to develop an optimistic mentality. Life coaches advise clients to focus on opportunities for growth rather than problems. This entails recasting problems as chances to learn and grow.

Positive affirmations, visualization exercises, and cultivating a positive mindset are all important components of staying motivated.

Accountability is critical in maintaining drive. Coaches assist clients in developing an accountability strategy, whether through frequent check-ins, journaling, or collaboration with an accountability buddy. Knowing that someone cares about their accomplishment inspires people to keep on course and endure in the face of adversity.

Life coaches often highlight the significance of passion and harmony with personal beliefs. Pursuing objectives that align with one's passions and beliefs creates intrinsic motivation, increasing the likelihood that people will stay committed in the long run. Identifying and engaging with these underlying motives aids in maintaining excitement and commitment.

Finally, life coaches frequently use the notion of incentives in goal-setting processes. Celebrating accomplishments of any size fosters healthy behavior. Whether it's a tiny indulgence or recognizing progress with a sense of success, incentives generate a positive feedback loop that fosters continued motivation.

Developing Resilience In The Face Of Adversity

Setbacks are an unavoidable part of every trip, and developing resilience is an important component of overcoming obstacles and maintaining progress. Life coaches help people develop resilience, which allows them to recover from setbacks and keep advancing toward their objectives.

Fostering a growth mindset is an important part of developing resilience. Setbacks are viewed as chances for learning and progress by those who have a growth mentality, rather than as insurmountable failures. Life coaches assist clients in redefining their perceptions of failures, urging them to see difficulties as stepping stones toward achievement.

Another essential component of resilience is self-awareness. Coaches assist individuals in comprehending their reactions to setbacks, assisting them in identifying patterns of thought or behavior that may impede growth. Self-aware individuals are better able to respond to setbacks in a more productive and adaptable manner.

Building resilience requires incorporating flexibility into goal-setting. When faced with unanticipated hurdles, life coaches urge their clients to remain adaptive and open to changing their plans. This adaptability enables the investigation of alternate paths to goals, preventing setbacks from derailing the entire journey.

A solid support system is an essential component of resilience. Life coaches help people find and nurture relationships with people who offer support, wisdom, and understanding during difficult times.

A dependable support network boosts resilience by providing a sense of connection and shared experiences.

Mindfulness activities can also help you build resilience. Meditation, deep breathing, and mindfulness exercises all help people stay anchored in the present moment. They can handle stress, control emotions, and tackle setbacks with a calm and focused mentality thanks to these habits.

Celebrating accomplishment, no matter how modest is a crucial resilience-building tactic. Life coaches help people recognize and appreciate their accomplishments, emphasizing the concept that setbacks are transient and part of the broader journey.

This positive reinforcement helps to foster a robust mindset capable of weathering the storms of adversity.

Investigating Various Life-Coaching Approaches

Life coaching is a dynamic profession that includes several techniques that are suited to the requirements and aspirations of the individual. Understanding and experimenting with various life coaching styles may improve the efficacy of the coaching process and adapt to a wide range of client preferences.

The solution-focused coaching paradigm is one such method. This method focuses on discovering and implementing solutions to specific problems. Coaches who use this model assist clients in clarifying their goals, exploring viable solutions, and developing practical steps. The emphasis is on the present and future, with less attention on previous obstacles.

Transformational coaching is another common technique. This strategy focuses on personal development and self-discovery to achieve substantial and long-term transformation. Transformational coaches help people explore their values, beliefs, and purpose, resulting in a better knowledge of themselves and their objectives.

Behavioral coaching is concerned with modifying specific habits to attain desired results. This strategy involves coaches working with clients to identify patterns of behavior that may be impeding growth and developing solutions to improve these habits. The emphasis is on achieving meaningful, quantifiable outcomes through behavioral change.

Coaching that integrates cognitive and behavioral techniques to address attitudes, beliefs, and actions is known as cognitive-behavioral coaching. Coaches assist clients in identifying and changing negative thinking patterns and behaviors that may be impeding their growth. By targeting both cognitive and behavioral components of human growth, this strategy strives to achieve long-term change.

Holistic coaching takes into account the full person, acknowledging the interdependence of multiple life areas. Coaches who use this technique analyze the physical, emotional, social, and spiritual components of a person's life to develop a holistic coaching plan. For total well-being, holistic coaching stresses balance and integration.

Narrative coaching is concerned with the tales people tell themselves about their lives. Coaches assist clients in exploring and reshaping their narratives to develop empowered and positive tales. This method acknowledges the influence of personal narratives on beliefs, attitudes, and behaviors.

Co-active coaching is a collaborative technique in which the coach and client work as equal partners in the coaching relationship.

Co-active coaches guide clients to uncover their answers and take action, facilitating a dynamic process of self-discovery. The emphasis is on collaboratively developing a coaching partnership that empowers the client.

The best coaching approach is determined by the individual's preferences, goals, and the nature of the coaching relationship.

Life coaches frequently combine components from multiple systems to create a personalized coaching experience that meets the specific requirements of each client.

CHAPTER FIVE

Including Mindfulness And Well-Being In Goal-Setting

Mindfulness, or being completely present and aware at the moment, has grown in popularity in a variety of disciplines, including life coaching.

Incorporating mindfulness into goal-setting improves self-awareness, emotional control, and general well-being. Life coaches employ mindfulness practices to assist clients in developing a focused and balanced approach to accomplishing their objectives.

The development of present-moment awareness is a vital part of integrating mindfulness. Coaches help people pay attention to their ideas, emotions, and bodily experiences without passing judgment. This knowledge enables clients to make deliberate decisions that are in line with their goals, encouraging a more conscious and meaningful way of living.

Before defining targets, mindful goal planning requires understanding values and priorities. Coaches help clients to uncover their deepest desires, ensuring that their objectives reflect their true selves. By tying goals to a feeling of purpose and meaning, this method increases motivation and commitment.

Meditation and deep breathing are two mindfulness activities that help with emotional control. Coaches educate people on how to manage tension, worry, and other emotions that may emerge when pursuing their goals. This emotional resilience improves the capacity to deal with obstacles and failures in a calm and focused manner.

Mindful activity stresses being completely focused on the present moment while working toward goals. Coaches help people break down activities into smaller, more manageable steps and encourage them to approach each activity with full concentration and intention. This thoughtful approach promotes a sense of success and happiness in the goal-achieving process.

Another key component is mindful reflection. Coaches urge clients to reflect on their successes, difficulties, and insights frequently. This introspective exercise increases self-awareness, allowing individuals to make necessary changes to their objectives and techniques. Mindful reflection also allows you to recognize your accomplishments and show thanks for the trip.

Mindfulness efforts are supplemented by including well-being techniques in the coaching process. Life coaches understand the interdependence of physical, mental, and emotional well-being in goal attainment. To support general well-being, strategies for maintaining a healthy lifestyle, such as exercise, diet, and enough sleep, are incorporated into the coaching plan.

Using Goal Setting To Navigate Life Transitions

Transitions are common in life, whether they include work changes, relationship changes, or personal adjustments. Using goal planning to navigate these changes gives individuals a feeling of direction and purpose during times of change. Life coaches play an important role in guiding people through transitions and assisting them in setting meaningful objectives for the next chapter of their lives.

Individuals may suffer ambiguity and a sense of loss during times of transition. Life coaches help clients articulate their beliefs, goals, and vision for the future. This method assists individuals in gaining a better grasp of themselves and their goals for the next stage of their lives.

To navigate life changes, it is critical to set realistic and achievable objectives. Coaches help clients set short- and long-term objectives that are in line with their beliefs and priorities. These objectives function as anchors, offering a feeling of structure and purpose while people negotiate the uncertainties of transition.

Adapting to change necessitates resilience, and life coaches assist individuals in developing resilience during times of transition. The coaching approach incorporates strategies for stress management, coping mechanisms development, and keeping a positive mentality. Coaches often stress the value of self-care and well-being activities in helping people negotiate life changes.

During life changes, goal setting becomes a tool for empowerment. Transitions are viewed as chances for personal and professional progress by coaches. Setting and attaining objectives during these times not only gives a sense of success, but also encourages a proactive and hopeful attitude in the face of change.

Developing a strategic action plan is an important part of handling life transitions and goal setting. Coaches assist customers in breaking down bigger goals into smaller, manageable actions. This step-by-step method makes the process more manageable and helps people to make continuous progress toward their goals even while things are changing.

During life transitions, it is critical to establish a support network. Coaches help clients find friends, family, mentors, and other resources that can offer advice and support. Having a support system makes people feel more connected and helps them negotiate obstacles more efficiently.

Flexibility is a critical component of goal-setting throughout life changes. Coaches stress the significance of modifying objectives and techniques as circumstances change. Individuals who are open to reassessing and altering goals can remain nimble and sensitive to the dynamic nature of life transitions.

Finally, life coaching provides individuals with useful skills and techniques for defining goals, building resilience, and navigating many parts of life. The concepts of life coaching allow individuals to live meaningfully and honestly, whether they are focused on retaining motivation, overcoming setbacks, exploring multiple coaching styles, incorporating mindfulness, or managing life changes. Individuals may unleash their full potential, achieve their goals, and live satisfying lives with the help of expert coaches.

Conclusion

The culmination of life coaching and goal setting is a celebration of transformation and empowerment. As a dynamic process, life coaching guides individuals through self-discovery, assists them in articulating their objectives, and provides a systematic path to accomplishing personal and professional goals. This trip concludes with a tremendous sense of accomplishment and self-awareness.

Goals are not only fulfilled but frequently exceeded, thanks to the joint efforts of the coach and the person. The approach instills a long-term mentality adjustment, encouraging resilience and adaptation in the face of adversity.

It becomes a positive transformation catalyst, generating a sense of purpose and fulfillment.

Individuals are now armed with a tailored toolset for continual self-improvement as a result of this finding. Goal setting, which was traditionally considered a difficult undertaking, becomes a skill polished via the coaching process. This conclusion is significant because of the ripple effect it causes, which extends beyond the initial aims specified. Individuals emerge not just with accomplishments, but also with fresh confidence, clarity, and a plan for future pursuits.

Life coaching and goal setting, when combined, give not just a means to an end, but a transforming journey that reshapes lives, with the conclusion marking the beginning of a new and empowered chapter.

THE END

www.ingramcontent.com/pod-product-compliance
Lightning Source LLC
Chambersburg PA
CBHW060847260726
48661CB00002B/648

9 798887 029165